# ISLE OF WIGHT MISCELLANY

# MISCELLANY

## by IAN WILLIAMS

with LINDA GOODWIN

# PUBLISHERS

Copyright ©
COACH HOUSE PUBLICATIONS LIMITED
2007

## BRITISH LIBRARY CATALOGUING IN PUBLICATION DATA

A catalogue record for this book is available from the British Library

ISBN: 978-1-899392-51-3
September 2007

*Published By*
COACH HOUSE PUBLICATIONS LIMITED,

ISLE OF WIGHT, ENGLAND
THE BEACON BUILDING, DAISH WAY,
NEWPORT,
ISLE OF WIGHT, PO30 5XJ
+44 (0)1983 533625

www.coachhousepublications.co.uk

BOOK DESIGN BY DAVID BOWLES

PRINTED IN THE UK

see more titles available from www.coachhousepublications.co.uk

# INTRODUCTION

## MISCELLANY

If you enjoy a tasty morsel rather than a heavy meal or prefer to skim through a magazine than wade through a novel then this is a book for you. It is designed for flickers and dippers, browsers who want to be taken by surprise. It is a book to begin not at the start but in the middle.

It is deliberately unorganised and unindexed to encourage skimming. It is designed for those looking not for enlightenment but entertainment. It is a drink to be sipped not quaffed.

It is not comprehensive but selective for there may be more to come. The criteria for inclusion is pure whim. Resident and visitor will find something to savour though it was designed for neither (or both) in mind. It is a mix of history and hearsay, fact and anecdote, information of little use other than to cause a wry smile, an expression of surprise or disbelief. Snippets to tuck away and recount to others later. We hope you will enjoy these nibbles!

# MISCELLANY

## ROYAL VISITS

Fifteen different monarchs have made visits to the Isle of Wight during their reign. In chronological order they are:-

ETHELRED THE UNREADY, CANUTE, HAROLD, JOHN, EDWARD I,
HENRY VII, HENRY VIII, JAMES I, CHARLES I, CHARLES II, VICTORIA,
EDWARD VII, GEORGE V, GEORGE VI, ELIZABETH II.

*A man driving a horse and cart drove by the County Asylum at Whitecroft one day. Beneath the cart hung a bucket to pick up horse droppings. The man stopped to put some droppings in the bucket when an inmate asked what he was going to do with them. "I shall take them home and put them on my rhubarb," said the man. "You ought to be in here," said the inmate. "We get custard."*

## HIRE OF CARRIAGES, 1860

|                    | *per mile* | *per hour* | *per day* |
|--------------------|------------|------------|-----------|
| One horse carriage | 1s 0d      | 2s 6d      | 15 – 18s  |
| Two horse carriage | 1s 6d      | 5s 0d      | 21s – 21 6d |
|                    |            |            | *according to distance* |

### DRIVER'S FEE

|                  |     |                    |       |
|------------------|-----|--------------------|-------|
| For a single horse | 3d  | 1s 0d first hour*  | 4s 0d |
| For a pair         | 4d  | 1s 0d each hour    | 5s 0d |

*6d each subsequent hour

1

"The Isle of Wight, from the variety it presents in point of elevation, soil, and aspect, and from the configuration of its hills and shores, possesses several peculiarities of climate and situation, which render it a favourable and commodious residence throughout the year, for a large class of invalids."

**Dr James Clark,** *Treatise on the Influence of Climate in the Cure of Chronic Diseases*

### Did you know
the exact centre of the island is at Shide Corner, SE of Newport?

## PIERS

| Date built | Pier | Length/ft | Lost |
|---|---|---|---|
| 1814 | Ryde | 2250 | standing |
| 1841 | Cowes Fountain | 100 | standing |
| 1864 | Ryde Tramway | 2,250 | 1969 |
| 1864 | Ryde Victoria | 970 | 1924 |
| 1864 | Ventnor Harbour | incomplete | 1867 |
| 1867 | Cowes Royal | 250 | 1876 |
| 1872 | 2nd Ventnor | 478 | 1881 |
| 1876 | Yarmouth | 685 | standing |
| 1879 | Sandown | 875 | standing |
| 1880 | Ryde Railway | 2,250 | standing |
| 1880 | Totland Bay | 450 | standing |
| 1881 | Seaview | 1,000 | 1950 |
| 1887 | Ventnor Royal Vic | 650 | 1950 |
| 1887 | Alum Bay | 370 | 1927 |
| 1890 | Shanklin | 1250 | 1987 |
| 1902 | Cowes Victoria | 170 | 1951 |
| 1955 | Ventnor New Royal Vic | 685 | 1993 |

The Nab Tower was designed as part of the anti-submarine defences across the Dover Straits during the first World War. Built in secrecy at Shoreham, the "Mystery Tower" was a steel tower on a concrete hull made from 100,000 concrete blocks weighing 9,000 tons. The end of the war made it a white elephant until Trinity House proposed using it to replace the Nab Lightship. On 12 September 1920 six tugs towed it the 41 miles to the Nab shoal where it was sunk by pouring liquid concrete to fill the holes in the blocks.

### Princess Beatrice's Isle of Wight Rifles
Officers Uniform Regulations
(excerpt from Battalion Standing Orders, April 1914)

FULL DRESS UNIFORM for Guard of Honour, Ceremonial and Church Parade. Green cloth tunic, overalls with mohair stripes, busby with plume and lines, cross belt and pouch, Blackweb sword belt with patent leather slings, Rifle pattern sword with nickeled scabbard and hilt, and black sword knot of flat patent leather, black Wellington boots, black gloves, and nickeled swan necked spurs for mounted officers.

The phrase to **"holystone the decks"** comes from the old Ship Commandment:

Six days shalt thou labour, and do all that thou art able,
And on the seventh, holystone the decks and scrape the cable

and originates from the days when the navy would anchor off St Helens to provision and drill before embarking on a journey. The crews would scrub the decks with sand and blocks of stone taken from the crumbling ruin of St Helens Church. These were called "holystones" larger blocks, and even tombstones, called "bibles" were hauled along the decks by ropes.

**Ryde Pier was Britain's first promenade pier and today is the third longest in Britain (after Southend and Southport)**

"One of the most attractive objects of a public kind is the pier. This ornament to the town . . . forms a beautiful marine promenade . . . Here hour after hour may be passed, without being sensible how rapidly time is gliding away."

**Horsey's** *Beauties of the Isle of Wight*, 1827

# YAVERLAND APPLE JELLY

(From John Smith's account book, Yaverland, c. 1836)

"Let the apples be pared, quartered, and freed from seed vessels, put them in an oven, in a pot without water, with a close lid. When the heat has made them soft, put them into a cloth, and wring out the juice. Put a little white of Egg into it. Add a little sugar. Skim it carefully before it boils. Reduce it to a proper consistency and you will have an excellent jelly."

**Did you know**

in the eighteenth century women who were in the workhouse for 'persistent bastardy' were required to wear bright yellow gowns?

In 1905, Charles Edgar of Ryde became the first island motorist to be convicted of drunken driving. He was fined £1 and had his licence suspended for three months.

# BAYS & COVES

## CLOCKWISE FROM EAST COWES

| | | | |
|---|---|---|---|
| Osborne Bay | Seagrove Bay | Priory Bay | Whitecliff Bay |
| Horseshoe Bay | Sandown Bay | Luccombe Bay | Steel Bay |
| Monks Bay | Horseshoe Bay | Wheelers Bay | Mill Cove |
| Ventnor Bay | Castle Cove | Steephill Cove | Orchard Bay |
| Mount Bay | Sir Richard's Cove | Woody Bay | Binnel Bay |
| Puckaster Cove | Reeth Bay | Watershoot Bay | Chale Bay |
| Fishing Cove | Brighstone Bay | Brook Bay | Compton Bay |
| | Freshwater Bay | Watcombe Bay | Scratchell's Bay |
| Alum Bay | Totland Bay | Colwell Bay | Newtown Bay |
| | Thorness Bay | Gurnard Bay | |

Sandown housewife Dorothy O'Grady became a household name when on 17 December 1940 she was sentenced to be hanged after being found guilty of offences under the Treachery Act. On appeal this was commuted to 14 years in prison and she served the full term in Holloway Prison.

## PORTERAGE CHARGES AT RYDE PIER, 1834

| | |
|---|---|
| Barrow load to Lower Ryde | 1s 0d |
| Single trunk, or parcel, to ditto | 0s 3d |
| Small parcel to ditto | 0s 2d |
| Barrow load to Upper Ryde, as far as the Star Inn | 1s 6d |
| Single trunk, or parcel, to ditto | 0s 6d |
| Small parcel to ditto | 0s 3d |

### PIER DUES, IN ADDITION TO THE ABOVE, ARE:

| | |
|---|---|
| For each barrow load | 0s 6d |
| Single trunk, or parcel, each | 0s 2d |

(from John Mackett, The Portsmouth-Ryde Passage)

*Pebbling was a popular Victorian seaside pastime and on Ventnor's shingle beach could be found pebbles of jasper, agate and rock crystal (known as Isle of Wight Diamonds). Collectors were warned against commercial agates from Germany masquerading as Isle of Wight agates. These worthless specimens came from South America, as ship ballast, to Germany where they were artificially brightened by heating and stained with acids.*

### Did you know

until enlarged in 1842 by the first Lord Yarborough, St Lawrence church, measuring just 20 feet by 11 feet by 6 feet to the eaves, was the smallest church in all England?

Air raid sirens sounded a total of **1,594** times during the Second World War, including on **55** consecutive days and nights between 18 March and 11 May 1941. A total of **214** islanders died in air raids and **274** suffered serious injuries. **10,873** buildings were destroyed or damaged. In **125** air raids **1,748** high explosive bombs and landmines fell on the island, in addition to thousands of incendiaries and oil bombs and **6** 'doodlebugs.'

ALBERT MIDLANE *was born at Carisbrooke on 23 January 1825, son of an ironmonger. At 17 he composed his first hymn and went on to write over one thousand. His hymn, "There's a Friend for little children," proved universally popular and on its jubilee three thousand children sang it at St Paul's Cathedral before the composer himself, a tribute accorded no other English hymn-writer.*

**Did you know**
Newport's main streets were lit by electricity for the first time on New Year's Day, 1903.

*There are* *1,383* *individually numbered footpaths, bridleways and byways recorded on the Definitive Map. These are identified by over*

*2,000* *signposts.*

Many years ago an old lady was looking over a cottage in Chillerton with a view to buying when she noticed there was no lock on the outside toilet. The owner said, "Well I've been here forty years and nobody's nicked the bucket yet!"

*The first fatal air crash on the Isle of Wight was a double tragedy claiming the lives of two brothers. On 7 September 1916 Ralph Lashmar was at the controls of a White's Landplane Bomber prototype with his brother Allan as observer when the machine went out of control and crashed near Cockleton Lane, Gurnard killing Ralph instantly. Allan died shortly after. The brothers are buried at Whippingham churchyard, the broken propeller their tombstone.*

The term **"milking the harrow"** meaning to do something that is pointless derived from agricultural practice. When harrowing the land, if the tines get clogged with vegetation and wet earth then the ground is too wet for the task.

*"She thinks of nothing but the Isle of Wight, and she calls it 'the island', as if there were no other island in the world."*

Jane Austen, *Mansfield Park*

# A SELECTION OF WORDS PECULIAR TO THE ISLE OF WIGHT DIALECT.

**Binder**
a large quantity, generally of food

**Dollurs**
lowness of spirit

**Dover, Duver**
a sandy piece of waste near the sea

**Dwyes**
currents or eddies

**Flanyer**
to flourish or brandish

**Halped**
crippled

**Hurdleshell**
tortoiseshell, used of colour

**Jingum bob**
a knick knack

**Luck**
a pool of water left among the rocks by the receding tide

**Mit**
a maggot

**Mudd**
a silly, thoughtless, stupid person

**Muggleton**
an old island name for a rat

**Nubby Joe**
a walking stick with a large knob at the end

**Pokeassen about**
to pry. Also to fritter away time to no purpose

**Rounty**
rough, as applied to marshes only
**Scoggel**
to eat voraciously; to gulp down
**Shroke**
shrivelled
**Sletch**
to stop; to cease
**Snobble**
to devour greedily; to snap up
**Twickered out**
tired out, weary
**Wobblejaad**
rickety, shaky

# DR. WILLIAMSON'S CHRISTMAS CAKE

(Dr Williamson was a Ventnor doctor who attended upon Karl Marx and a young Winston Churchill on their visits to the island).

1/2lb butter, 1/2lb sugar (granulated or soft brown), 3/4lb self-raising flour, 2lb fruit (sultanas and stoneless raisins), 3 eggs, 1/2 teaspoon vanilla essence, 1/2 teaspoon almond essence, 2oz cherries, wineglass of sherry, a little milk. Crumble the butter into the flour, add the sugar, then the eggs. Put in the fruit and mix well. Finally, add the sherry and flavourings. Put thick layers of greaseproof paper (or foil) inside the tin before adding the cake mixture. The tin should be greased with lard. Cook for three hours at 325F, Mark 3, and leave the cake to cool in the tin.

**Did you know**

it has been calculated that the East Yar river flows into Bembridge harbour at an average rate of 13,200,000 gallons per day?

*Born at Whippingham on 17 January 1878, CLEMENT LESLIE SMITH won the **Victoria Cross** as a Lieutenant in the Duke of Cornwall's Light Infantry when, on 10 January 1904, he made a brave, determined rescue of a hospital assistant beleagured by dervishes at Jidbaldi, Somaliland.*

**The worst snowstorm to hit the island occurred between 18 – 21 January 1881 when level snow three feet deep was recorded and drifts, driven by fierce winds, reached the rooftops at Ryde. One islander recalled "the snow fell for three days and nights and it froze so hard that people were able to walk on top of hedges."**

Sir Godfrey Baring's 51 years as Chairman of the Isle of Wight County Council remains an unrivalled record in English local government which is unlikely ever to be beaten. Dubbed "the Prime Minister of the island" Sir Godfrey was chairman from 1898 until 1949. He established three more records on becoming Island MP in 1906. He obtained the largest number of votes ever polled on the island up to that time, secured a larger majority than any previous island victor and in the House of Commons that year was the only member not to miss a single one of the 636 divisions!

To be **"under the clock"** was a euphemism for being confined in the County Asylum at Whitecroft and refers to the bell-tower which featured a clock with two dials.

# RAILWAYS TIMETABLE

| Line | Operator | Opened | Closed |
|---|---|---|---|
| Cowes–Newport | IWCR | 16 June 1862 | 1966 |
| Ryde St Johns-Shanklin | IWR | 23 Aug 1864 | |
| Shanklin-Ventnor | IWR | 10 Sept 1866 | 1966 |
| Sandown-Newport (Shide) | IWCR | 1 Feb 1875 | 1956 |
| Shide-Pan Lane ext | IWCR | 6 Oct 1875 | 1956 |
| Ryde-Newport | IWCR | 20 Dec 1875 | 1966 |
| Pan Lane-Newport | IWCR | 1 June 1879 | 1956 |
| Ryde St Johns-Pierhead | L&SWR/LB&SCR | 12 July 1880 | |
| Brading-Bembridge | IWR | 27 May 1882 | 1952 |
| Freshwater-Newport | FY&NR | 20 July 1889 | 1953 |
| Merstone-St Lawrence | IWCR | 20 July 1897 | 1952 |
| St Lawrence-Ventnor West | IWCR | 1 June 1900 | 1952 |

KEY:

| | |
|---|---|
| **IWCR** | Isle of Wight Central Railway |
| **IWR** | Isle of Wight Railway |
| **FY&NR** | Freshwater, Yarmouth and Newport Railway |
| **L&SWR** | London and South Western Railway |
| **LB&SCR** | London, Brighton and South Coast Railway |

In 1923 all railway companies were absorbed by Southern Railway. In 1948 SR became the Southern Region of British Railways.

**Did you know**
that because of the short duration of his reign there are only
two Edward VIII pillar post-boxes on the island, at Green Lane,
Shanklin and Melville Street, Sandown?

**Dave Hunnybun of Cowes was the first birdwatcher to observe 200 different species in one calendar year, reaching a total of 204 species in 2002. "I don't advise anybody to try this unless they are retired, have an understanding wife and a car that does 80 miles to the gallon."**

*In May 1952 the 69 members of the
I.W. Meat Traders Association having their
annual outing at Bath lunched out on fried Spam
due to a meat shortage.*

**Did you know**
the most unusual fossil to be found at island coasts is crocodile poo?
Croissant-shaped fossilized crocodile droppings containing fish
remains can be found off Hamstead beach.

# *Pop Singer*

## CRAIG DOUGLAS,

real name Terry Perkins, was born on the Isle of Wight on 12 August 1941, moving to London in the mid-50s. While working on the island as a milkman he got the opportunity to appear on TV's 'Six-5 Special' by winning a talent contest. This secured him a recording contract with Decca but his first two singles flopped. A second chance came with a move to Top Rank where he was very successful recording covers of American artists. He had a No.1 hit with Sam Cooke's 'Only Sixteen' and co-starred with Helen Shapiro in the 1961 film *It's Trad Dad.* He had four further Top Ten hits but by 1964 the Beat boom effectively ended his chart career. It was groups like the Beatles, who backed Craig on their first major stage show, who eroded Craig's popularity. He continues to this day on the cabaret and nostalgia circuit.

## QUOTE UNQUOTE

" . . . THAT BEAUTIFUL ISLAND, WHICH HE WHO
HAS ONCE SEEN NEVER FORGETS, THROUGH
WHATEVER PART OF THE WIDE WORLD HIS FUTURE
PATH MAY CARRY HIM."

**Sir Walter Scott,** *The Surgeon's Daughter*

The island measures **23** miles east to west and **13** miles north
to south with **57** miles of coastline of which **28** miles are designated Heritage Coast. It has a land area of **146.8** square miles
(38,014 hectares) of which **73.5** square miles (19,038 hectares)
are designated Areas of Outstanding Natural Beauty (AONB)
and **11.9** square miles (3,072 hectares) are designated Sites of
Special Scientific Interest (SSSIs).

*The Isle of Wight has 133 churches of 15 different
denominations. The most numerous are Church of England with
56 churches followed by the Methodists with 29.*

**Did you know**

the Glanville Fritillary butterfly can be found on the slumped
cliffs of the 'back of the Wight' and nowhere else in Britain? It was
named after Lady Eleanor Glanville in the 18th century whose
hobby of collecting butterflies was cited as grounds of insanity
when her will was contested.

## CROSSROADS ON THE ISLAND ARE CALLED SIMPLY CROSS AND THERE ARE 22 OF THESE:

Alverstone    Arreton    Beckfield    Branstone
Bullen    Crouchers    Fighting Cocks    Knights    Leechmore
Little Princelett    Lynn    Merstone    Shide    Steyne    Stocks
Upton    Vittlefields    Whitcombe    Whitehouse    Willets
Winford    Wroxall

In 1943 the Germans began dropping bombs filled with Colorado beetles over the island to try and destroy the potato crop. Teams of evacuee schoolchildren were used to round them up.

The eighteenth century English radical journalist and politician John WILKES is credited with having 'discovered' Sandown. He built a cottage, which he called his villakin, when the only other buildings were the fort and barracks. When his friend, the poet and satirist Charles Churchill died, Wilkes erected a Doric column in the grounds of his cottage, the base of which was kept stocked with port in the poet's honour. The inscription read "To the divine poet, the genial friend, the citizen deserving of his country's highest regard." Neither cottage nor column remain but a plaque on a wall in Wilkes Road, Sandown (GR598842) marks the site.

In the Shipping Forecast the borders of sea area **WIGHT** are from Beachy Head to Dieppe in the east and Hengistbury Head to Cherbourg in the west.

**The first recorded (but unplanned) cross-Solent flight was on 3 August 1909 when Messrs Singer and Pollack got blown across in a balloon to Cowes.**

*King Henry V was the first English monarch to gather his fleet for a formal inspection. It was in 1415 as he prepared to sail to France for a campaign culminating at Agincourt. Since then there have been 43 royal naval reviews, the last in 1977 for the Queen's Silver Jubilee. All but two – those in 1919 and 1965 – were held at the Spithead anchorage. The largest was the review of the D-Day invasion fleet in May 1944 when King George VI saw 800 vessels ranging from battleships to small minesweepers and landing craft. An International Fleet Review with over 100 ships from dozens of countries was held in the Solent in June 2005.*

*On Friday 23 August 1940 55yr old Edith Clarke was killed by a bomb whilst drinking tea in a beach hut at Sandown. Ironically, she left her North London home and moved to her sister's house in Sandown to escape the London air raids.*

In what proved to be the first commercial flight to the island, the Daily Mail chartered a Handley Page bomber on 8 May 1919 to parachute newspapers into south coast towns. The bundles destined for Ryde pierhead landed in the sea!

*The Isle of Wight County in Virginia, USA, was one of the original eight shires of America. It is roughly the size of the island and remarkably similar in shape to the island's outline!*

**The Rev William Fox, curate of Brighstone, discovered more species of dinosaur than anyone else in the UK and has more dinosaurs named after him than any other Englishman.**

Three brothers from the Isle of Wight were killed on the same day in the same battle during the Gallipoli campaign in the First World War. **Edward George Urry, William Henry Urry** and **Frederick Albert Urry** were killed on 12 August 1915 as the Isle of Wight Rifles attacked the Turkish lines across the Anafarta Plain.

### Did you know

82 species of vascular plants have become extinct on the island between 1850 and 2000, a rate of one species every two years?

---

**Forest House puddens** were puddings made of flour and suet, which were supplied to the inmates of the workhouse, or House of Industry, at Parkhurst, for dinner on Saturdays. They contained neither raisins, currants nor sugar and were not much liked.

*"We intend no disrespect to the finest town in the island in saying, generally speaking, people go to Ryde to get away from it."*

**Ward Lock's Guide**

# SAILING CLUBS AND THEIR BURGEES

| Club | Established | Burgee |
|---|---|---|
| Bembridge S.C. | 1886 | white with blue border round two sides opposite hoist, red map of IW inside |
| Brading Haven Y.C. | 1950 | bishop's yellow mitre on blue background |
| Cowes Corinthian Y.C. | 1953 | red with facsimile of 17th century ship, the Ark |
| East Cowes S.C. | 1912 | blue castle in centre of white cross on red background |
| Gurnard S.C. | 1931 | blue with yellow cross and Gurnard in top recovery |
| Island S.C. | 1889 | red with yellow castle superimposed |
| Royal Corinthian Y.C. | 1872 | blue with gold laurel wreath and centre crown |
| Royal London Y.C | 1838 | blue with city of London shield and gold crown in the centre |
| Royal Solent Y.C. | 1878 | dark blue with Yarmouth Gallery surmounted by a crown |
| Royal Victoria Y.C. | 1844 | red with gold crown above fouled anchor and letters VR |
| Royal Yacht Squadron | 1815 | red St George Cross on white ground, gold crown in centre |
| Seaview Y.C. | 1893 | white with red border, two interlaced letter 'S's |
| Shanklin S.C. | 1932 | blue cross on white, blue boat in top left |
| Yarmouth S.C. | 1970 | two blue triangles at hoist end and a red Y on a white diamond |

*The first passenger train to run on the island left Cowes for Newport at 8.15 am on 16 June 1862 with just six passengers aboard.*

The twenty one volunteers from the Isle of Wight Rifles who went on active service during the Boer War as part of 2nd Battalion, Hampshire Regiment took part in the record march of the War covering the 35 miles from Pretoria to Uitvlie Nek in just over 12 hours.

*Eric Charles Twelves WILSON born at Sandown on 2nd October 1912 won the* **Victoria Cross** *as a Captain in the East Surrey Regiment, attached to the Somaliland Camel Corps. He won it on 11-15 August 1940 at Observation Hill, Somaliland (now Somalia) by keeping a machine gun post in action in spite of being wounded.*

### Did you know

the total resident population of the I.W. in 2001 was 132,731 of which 63,697 were males and 69,034 were females?

There were no badgers on the island until the 1920s when John Willis Fleming, Master of the Isle of Wight Hunt, imported a dozen animals in response to an outbreak of mange which threatened the fox population. The badgers drove the foxes from their diseased earths and cleaned them and the foxes dug new earths.

**LORD YARBOROUGH** *was the Royal Yacht Squadron's first Commodore and under his guidance the club became the unquestioned leader of yachting in the world. On his death in 1846 members erected a monument to him on Culver Down.*

*He was a great seaman and a generous host. His full-rigged ship, the 351 ton Falcon, was "not unlike a 20-gun ship of war" according to one observer. Indeed, her captain was a Naval Lieutenant and she was manned by a crew of 54 choice hands who voluntarily placed themselves under naval discipline for an extra shilling a week. He greatly encouraged cruising and it became common practice to cross the Channel to France or Spain to load up with wine for the coming season. Less serious sailors, dubbed 'Nab Nelsons', cruised the Solent then attended functions given by Lord Yarborough at his mansion at Appuldurcombe where hundreds of guests would enjoy a night of dancing and fireworks.*

*Lord Yarborough entertained on board, too, in lavish style. In 1827 whilst cruising the Mediterranean he became involved in the Battle of Navarino. The Admiral of the fleet, wishing to be rid of his Lordship, asked to use the Falcon as a dispatch vessel and sent him off with a message for the captain of a frigate sailing away from the fleet. It read: "Give his Lordship a good meal and he'll give you a better one in return."*

## WORLD MARBLES ON SAND CHAMPIONSHIPS

In June 2001 the island hosted the local heats and the National Finals of this unique event. An island policeman carried off the National Title and went to France to participate in the World Finals finishing in a very respectable 3rd place.

# HOUSEBOAT NAMES AT BEMBRIDGE

Rubstone    Day Dawn    Sea Horse    Petrenda    Pisces
Heyvon Harbour Lights    Emily    Merlin    Harmony    Fortune
Zambezi    Bryther II    Mark's Ark    Little Susie    Little Broom
Xoron Floatel    Freebird    Watershed    Myosotis    Gypsy Queen
Sirius & Blackrock

There are 827 km (514 miles) of public rights of way on the island including 266 km (165 miles) of bridleways and 47 km (29 miles) of byways. At 2.14 km of rights of way per square kilometre, the Isle of Wight network is the most concentrated network of rights of way in the country.

# DINOSAURS ONLY FOUND ON THE ISLAND

| | |
|---|---|
| YAVERLANDIA | *Jutish lizard* |
| IUTICOSAURUS | |
| EOTYRANNUS | *Earlier tyrannosaurus* |
| THECOCOELURUS | *Sheath hollow form* |
| CALAMOSPONDYLUS | *Reed vertebrae* |
| CALAMOSAURUS foxii | *Reed lizard* |
| ORNITHODESMUS | *Bird linked* |

### Did you know

the island's first hospital was the Leper Hospital at Gunville in the 13th century associated with the St Augustine Priory at Carisbrooke? The first general hospital was built at Ryde and opened in November 1849 with 25 beds.

# QUEEN VICTORIA'S CHILDREN

At Osborne House, Queen Victoria's island residence you can see the plaster cast hands and feet of her children.

PRINCESS *Victoria*
1840-1901

PRINCE *Edward*  Later King Edward VII
1841-1910

PRINCESS *Alice*
1842-1878

PRINCE *Alfred*
1844-1900

PRINCESS *Helena*
1846-1923

PRINCESS *Louise*
1848-1939

PRINCE *Arthur*
1850-1942

PRINCE *Leopold*
1853-1884

PRINCESS *Beatrice*
1857-1944

*Harry Frederick WHITCHURCH, born at Sandown on 22nd September 1866, won the **Victoria Cross** on 3rd March 1895 at the siege of Chitral Fort while serving as Surgeon-Captain in the Indian Medical Service, Chitral, NW Frontier. He went to the aid of Capt Baird, retrieving his body with the help of Ghurkas.*

J. Samuel White's of Cowes built 27 warships for the Royal Navy during the Second World war including **HMS Contest,** the world's first all-welded destroyer. A total of 21 submarine 'kills' were credited to Cowes-built warships.

*The biggest sailing ship to be wrecked on island shores was the 2,347 ton Irex, 302 feet long with masts 200 feet high. Amid accusations that her captain had gone mad, and of cowardice among the crew of the lifeboat that turned back, there was a dramatic rocket rescue and heroism by a rescued crewman who went back for the stranded ship's boy. It made the front page of The Illustrated London News.*

# ISLE OF WIGHT RAILWAY STATIONS

| Station | Opened | Closed |
|---|---|---|
| | FRESHWATER, YARMOUTH & NEWPORT RAILWAY | |
| Freshwater | 10 Sept 1888 | 21 Sept 1953 |
| Yarmouth | " | " |
| Ningwood | " | " |
| Calbourne & Shalfleet | " | " |
| Upper Watchingwell | " | " |
| Carisbrooke | " | " |
| Newport (FY&NR) | 1 July 1913 | Mar 1914 |
| | ISLE OF WIGHT CENTRAL RAILWAY | |
| Newport | 16 June 1862 | 21 Feb 1966 |
| Cement Mills Halt | " | " |
| Medina Wharf Halt | " | " |
| Mill Hill | " | " |
| Cowes | " | " |
| Whippingham | 20 Dec 1875 | 21 Sept 1953 |
| Wootton | " | " |
| Havenstreet | " | 21 Feb 1966 |
| Ashey | " | " |
| Pan Lane | 6 Oct 1875 | 1 June 1879 |
| Blackwater | 1 Feb 1875 | 6 Feb 1956 |
| Shide | " | " |
| Merstone | " | " |
| Horringford | " | " |
| Newchurch | " | " |
| Alverstone | " | " |

| *Station* | *Opened* | *Closed* |
|---|---|---|
| *Godshill* | 20 July 1897 | 15 Sept 1952 |
| *Whitwell* | " | " |
| *St Lawrence* | " | " |
| *Ventnor West* | 1 June 1900 | " |

## ISLE OF WIGHT RAILWAY

| *Ryde Pier Head* | 12 July 1880 | |
|---|---|---|
| *Ryde Esplanade* | 5 Apr 1880 | |
| *Ryde St Johns Road* | 23 Aug 1864 | |
| *Brading* | " | |
| *St Helens* | 27 May 1882 | 21 Sept 1953 |
| *Bembridge* | " | " |
| *Sandown* | 23 Aug 1864 | |
| *Shanklin* | " | |
| *Wroxall* | 10 Sept 1866 | 18 Apr 1966 |
| *Ventnor* | " | " |

*"This island is a little paradise," wrote Karl Marx to Freidrich Engels in mid July 1894.*

### Did you know

the oldest sporting organisation on the island is the Isle of Wight Hunt dating from 1845 when Benjamin Cotton of Afton Manor founded the first pack of foxhounds? It is also the only island foxhunt in the world.

# MAIN CROSSING ROUTES TO THE ISLAND

| *Points of departure/arrival* | *Type of ferry* |
|---|---|
| PORTSMOUTH – RYDE | Passenger catamaran |
| PORTSMOUTH – FISHBOURNE | Car ferry |
| SOUTHSEA – RYDE | Passenger hovercraft |
| SOUTHAMPTON – WEST COWES | Passenger catamaran |
| SOUTHAMPTON – EAST COWES | Car ferry |
| LYMINGTON – YARMOUTH | Car ferry |

*The Isle of Wight House of Industry or Workhouse opened in 1774 and was a pioneer development designed to take the old, the infirm, the destitute and their children from all of the island's 28 parishes. It was capable of housing up to 700 people and, standing alone on the extreme eastern edge of Parkhurst Forest, it was the largest public building on the island. Its main feature was the 118 feet long dining room. In the manufactory the inmates produced sacks for grain and flour. The day's work was organised by the clanging of a bell. The bell rang at six to wake everyone and the doors were unlocked and they were locked again in summer at eight.*

The Isle of Wight has **492** miles of roads of which **76** miles are 'A' roads, **167.5** miles are other classified roads and **248.5** miles are unclassified roads.

*On 10th June 1971 Shide recorded 4.79 inches of rain and the rest of the island had similar downpours. "The deluge represented the equivalent of 40 million tons of water on the island's 94,000 acres – an inch of rain on an acre weighing 101 tons" (Hosking). It went on to become the wettest June at Ryde since 1870. On 30/31 July 1951 a thunderstorm released 2.43 inches of rain in just 45 minutes round midnight leading to severe flooding.*

**Did you know**

on an average summer Saturday in the 1930s over 36,000 passengers would pass through Ryde Pier and trains would leave the pier at the rate of one every ten minutes?

**The Isle of Wight attracts 2.5 million visitors each year who spend over £300 million in the local economy, supporting 1 in 4 island jobs.**

The fox was introduced to the island by Will Thatcher, a supporter of fox hunting on the mainland. In 1843 Will bought eight foxes from a dealer in Portsmouth and secretly released them at Newchurch. Will's father, Squire Thatcher of Wacklands, kept a pack of hounds for hunting hare and was livid when, at his next meet, his dogs put up a fox!

A CHINE IS A steep-sided, narrow ravine cut through coastal cliffs by a river or stream. The term chine, peculiar to Hampshire, Dorset and the Isle of Wight, derives from the Saxon 'cinan' meaning a gap or yawn. There are 19 chines on the island. They are, clockwise from Shanklin:-

Shanklin   Luccombe   Blackgang   Walpen   Ladder   Whale

Shepherds   Cowleaze   Barnes   Grange/Marsh   Chilton

Brook   Shippards   Compton   Alum Bay   Widdick   Colwell

Brambles   Linstone

---

The first enemy aircraft to crash on the island was a Stuka dive bomber which made a forced landing at St Lawrence Shute after being attacked by a Hurricane. It was on 8 August 1940 during the Battle of Britain and was the first Stuka to be captured more or less intact on English soil. The same day saw the first British fighter plane to crash land on the island come down at Ford Farm, Whitwell.

*Claude RAYMOND born at Mottistone on the 2nd October 1923 won the **Victoria Cross** at Talaku, Burma, (now Myanmar) on the 21st March 1945 as a Lieutenant in the Corps of Royal Engineers. He led an attack against an enemy detachment and refused all aid till his men were attended to. He died the next day, 22nd March 1945.*

In 1176 John Speed reported "it rained a shower of blood" for two hours around Newchurch. This was probably dust particles in raindrops similar to the estimated 5,000 tons of Sahara dust that fell on southern England, including the island, on 1 July 1968.

*The first fatal air crash involving a serving RAF pilot occurred on 17 August 1926. Three aircraft from Gosport air base flew over the island and encountered a bank of fog. When 26yr old Lt John Leslie Llewellyn-Rees took his plane lower to try and escape the fog he hit Hulverstone Down. It was three hours before he was found still strapped into his machine, killed by massive concussion from the impact, though the only bone broken was his nose.*

THE FIRST SCHEDULED AIR SERVICE to the island was the Spithead Air Ferry begun on 27 June 1932 operated by Portsmouth, Southsea and Isle of Wight Aviation Ltd using a Westland Wessex carrying up to nine passengers. There were four flights daily between Portsmouth and Barnsley Farm, Ryde.

### Did you know
deaths exceed births by approx 500 every year and population growth is sustained by net migration to the I.W.?

# THERE ARE 28 SHUTES ON THE ISLAND.

They are, in alphabetical order:

Alverstone    Alvington    Barrack    Beaper    Berry

Bonchurch    Brighstone    Blythe    Cheverton

Clatterford    Gusters    Hallets    Harding    Longlands

Long Lane    Loverstone    Marshcombe    Newchurch

Niton    Old    Poorhouse    Presford    Princelett

Pyle    Shorwell    St Lawrence    Stone    Windmill

# BAKED HERRINGS

(FROM THE KITCHENS OF NUNWELL HOUSE, HOME TO
THE OGLANDER FAMILY)

*Clean and prepare the fish. Season them well with Pepper and
Salt and cover them with an Equal Quantity of Port Wine and
Vinegar and bake them the Same Time as Household Bread
(in a hot oven, 425-450F, Mark 7, for 10-15 minutes).
You may add two or three Bay Leaves.*

## QUOTE UNQUOTE

"ONE NOTICEABLE FEATURE OF THE ISLAND IS THE
GENERAL ABSENCE OF VULGARITY AND THE
REFINEMENT OF ITS RESIDENTS AND VISITORS,
WHICH PROBABLY ARISES FROM THE SUBDUED
AND LOVELY CHARACTER OF ITS SCENERY AND
THE MILDNESS OF ITS CLIMATE, BUT PRINCIPALLY
FROM THE ARISTOCRATIC CHARACTER OF MANY OF
ITS VISITORS, THE PRESENCE OF ROYALTY AND THE
ABSENCE OF THE MANUFACTURING ELEMENT,
OWING TO THE DISTANCE FROM THE NOISE AND
SMOKE OF TOWN."

Jenkinson's *Practical Guide to the Isle of Wight,* 1875

THE PADDLE STEAMER *Medina,* built in 1822 by
Ratseys of Cowes for an island consortium headed by George
Ward, had a fair number of 'firsts' to her credit. She was the first
steamer to be built specially for Solent service, the first to call at
Jersey, the first to call at Guernsey, the first to be built by a local
shipbuilder and the first to operate an excursion cruise around
the Isle of Wight.

*In the eighteenth century failed Newport grocer Thomas Boulter turned highwayman in order to repay his debts, and decided to hold up the Salisbury Coach. A life on the open road suited Thomas better than the grocery trade so he took to the London road, once robbing three coaches within hailing distance of one another. When captured he was offered the chance to join the army but he found the discipline too harsh and deserted. He was finally caught at Bridport and sentenced to death at Winchester on 31st July 1778.*

One of the oldest and most famous paintings in the Cricket Memorial Gallery of the MCC at Lords is entitled "A cricket match at Brading circa 1780." It depicts a bowler with an underarm delivery and a batsman defending a two-stump wicket.

*The island's worst peacetime disaster occurred in November 1957 when a large flying boat crashed into a chalk pit at Shalcombe Farm near Calbourne. The plane, bound for Madeira from Southampton, burst into flames. Of 50 passengers and 8 crew, 43 died at the scene and a further 2 died in hospital.*

*In November 1953 a board of visiting magistrates sentenced a Parkhurst prisoner to six strokes of the cat o' nine tails for attacking a prison officer. This was the last recorded occasion of its use in Parkhurst. The last case of birching was at Camp Hill Prison in 1961.*

# SCRABBLERS

According to J.W. Spears a leading Scrabble commentator, there are more Scrabble players per head of population on the IW than anywhere else in the UK. The IW Matchplay Scrabble Weekend is one of Britain's largest and most popular Scrabble events of the year.

| I.O.W. MATCHPLAY WEEKEND | | MAIN EVENT WINNERS |
|---|---|---|
| *Year* | *Winner* | *Highest Islander* |
| 2000 | *Danny* Bekhor | *Noel* Turner (3rd) |
| 2001 | *Andrew* Perry | *Penny* Downer (4th) |
| 2002 | *Penny* Downer | *Penny* Downer |
| 2003 | *Sandie* Simonis | *Noel* Turner (9th) |
| 2004 | *Femi* Awowade | *Penny* Downer (12th) |
| 2005 | *Elie* Dangoor | *Noel* Turner (3rd) |

# GARLIC

The island harvests a large crop of garlic each year and is one of the UK's major producers of this spicy bulb. Garlic beer, garlic fudge as well as smoked garlic are available at the Garlic Festival which takes place in August. The air is heady with the pungent smell and garlic ice cream, which could be considered a step too far, is also available!

*In 1922 Parkhurst prisoner Edward Commy, 33, serving a ten-year sentence, tunnelled his way out of jail. He was free for 12 days during which he committed a series of daring burglaries.*

**Norman Derham of East Cowes won a £1,000 prize in 1926 for swimming the English Channel in 13 hours.**

Sensational headlines in the national dailies like 'Polio Isle' in the summer of 1950 killed off the post-war revival in the holiday trade. An outbreak of poliomyelitis saw 54 paralytic and 41 non-paralytic cases of polio and three deaths on the island. Swimming pools were closed, extra iron lungs were flown in and the re-opening of schools after the summer holidays was delayed.

*The Island's first independent county police force was established in 1890. The 47 strong force was headed by Superintendent James Duke who, seven years later, was sentenced to six weeks hard labour for maliciously cutting a plane tree in Hope Road, Shanklin!*

**In 1895 John Morgan, serving 10 years for burglary, escaped from Parkhurst Prison but was recaptured in a boat off Cowes wearing stolen clerical garb.**

A bronze plaque on Cowes Parade was unveiled in 1933 to commemorate the sailing, 300 years before, of the ships Ark and Dove with the first British settlers for Maryland, USA.

*In 1887 oil lighting at St Catherine's Lighthouse was superseded by six million candlepower electric lighting.*

RYDE is the cradle of carnivals in this country by holding the first ever parade in 1888. Until then fairs and regattas were the main attractions but the Victorians craved something more as the island developed as a holiday resort. The carnival gained royal approval the following year when the Queen watched from a horse-drawn carriage by the Town Hall.

*In the early 1870s a curate at St Mary's Church, Cowes, the Rev Mr Hollis, is attributed with having started organising the first soccer matches. From such beginnings sprang Cowes FC in 1882, the first club of which there is any official record. In their first year they played no matches because there were no other teams!*

The Isle of Wight is recognised as one of the best places in Europe for dinosaur remains. 26 species have been found on the island and several have been found nowhere else in the world.

# ISLAND 'DOWNS'

A 'down' is an expanse of rolling grassy chalk upland in southern England. The chalk ridge that forms the backbone of the island from Culver Down to the Needles has 39 named downs along its length. From east to west they are:-

Culver    Bembridge    Nunwell    Brading    Ashey
Mersley    Arreton    St Georges    Pan    Garstons
Newbarn    Chillerton    Duken    Westridge    Northcourt
Idlecombe    Bowcombe    Apesdown    Little Down
Rowborough    Renham    Fore    Cheverton
Limerstone    Newbarn    Brighstone    Westover
Mottistone    Chessell    Pay    Shalcombe    Brook
Wellow    Tapnell    Compton    East Afton    Afton
Tennyson    West High Down

# BEACH HUTS

THERE ARE
56 BEACH HUTS
ON ST HELEN'S DUVER,
NUMBERED 1 UP
TO 28 AND THEN
28 DOWN TO 1

# EDWARD VII'S GIFT

EDWARD VII presented Osborne House at East Cowes to the nation in 1904. Osborne had been Victoria and Albert's beloved retreat from the bustle of court life in London. Why their eldest son disliked it so much is uncertain as he had spent much of his childhood there. Perhaps it was the isolation; he loved high society, and the remoteness of Osborne House made it unsuitable for the entertaining and socialising that appealed to the King.

# HOLIDAY WEATHER

**Driest months**    April-May-July
**Wettest months**    January-November-December
**Sunniest months**    May-July-August
**Dullest months**    January-November-December
**Warmest months**    June-July-August
**Coldest months**    January-February-December

TAKEN FROM THE 30 YEAR AVERAGES FROM 1969-1998

# OFFICIAL ISLE OF WIGHT HOLIDAY GUIDE 1982

*"One marvels, again and again, at the peaceful beauty and delights of this wonderful island. It seems that about a million other people think the same........."*

## WIND SPEEDS AT SEA

ONE OF THE FIRST SCALES TO ESTIMATE WIND SPEEDS AND THEIR EFFECTS WAS CREATED BY BRITAIN'S ADMIRAL SIR FRANCIS BEAUFORT (1774-1857).

HE DEVELOPED A SCALE IN 1805 TO HELP SAILORS ESTIMATE THE WINDS VIA VISUAL OBSERVATIONS. THE SCALE STARTS AT 0 AND GOES TO FORCE 12

0 1 2 3 4 5 6 7 8 9 10 11 12

# BEAUFORT SCALE FOR USE AT SEA

## 0 - CALM
*Sea like a mirror*

## 1 - LIGHT AIR
*Ripples with the appearance of scales*

## 2 - LIGHT BREEZE
*Small wavelets*

## 3 - GENTLE BREEZE
*Large wavelets, crest begins to break*

## 4 - MODERATE BREEZE
*Small waves becoming larger; fairly frequent white horses*

## 5 - FRESH BREEZE
*Moderate waves; pronounces long form; chance of spray*

## 6 - STRONG BREEZE
*Long waves; white foam crests are extensive*

## 7 - NEAR GALE
*Sea heaps up and white foam is blown in direction of the wind*

## 8 - GALE
*Moderately high waves of greater length; foam blown in well-marked streaks*

## 9 - SEVERE GALE
*High waves; crests of waves begin to topple, tumble and roll over*

## 10 - STORM
*Very high waves; the `tumbling` of the sea becomes heavy and shock-like; visibility affected*

## 11 - VIOLENT STORM
*Exceptionally high waves; small and medium sized ships might be lost from view for a time; the sea covered in foam.*

## 12 - HURRICANE
*The air is filled with foam and spray; visibility very seriously affected*

# ROBERT LORAINE

IN AUGUST 1910 ROBERT LORAINE BECAME THE FIRST AIRPLANE PILOT TO LAND ON THE ISLE OF WIGHT. HE WAS TAKING PART IN A BOURNEMOUTH FLYING MEETING WHEN RISING WINDS BLEW HIM OFF COURSE AND HE WAS FORCED TO LAND HIS HENRY FARMAN BI-PLANE ON THE NEEDLES GOLF COURSE. DAYS LATER WHEN THE STORM ABATED HIS FUEL WAS TOO LOW FOR A SAFE RETURN SO HE SENT HIS FRENCH MECHANIC VEDRINES TO THE MAINLAND TO OBTAIN PETROL AND THE SPECIAL OIL USED BY THE ENGINE. HE THEN TOOK OFF FROM THE THIRD GREEN.

# MOONFLEET

*"The wind set us up Channel, and by daybreak they put us ashore at Cowes, so we walked to Newport and came there before many were stirring"*

So wrote John Mead Falkner in his adventure novel ***"Moonfleet"***. His vivid imagination had his heroes John Trenchard and Elzevir Block heading into Cowes aboard the Bonaventure enroute for Carisbrooke Castle. They were in search of the Mohune Diamond and had decoded clues from the Psalms, inscribed on a parchment John had found in the Mohune Vault. The clues led them to the Well House at Carisbrooke Castle where, overseen by the suspicious turnkey who kept the Well House, they prepared to descend into the well.

*"We will let an end of this down the well" Elzevir said untwining a coil of rope from his arm. "This lad thinks the treasure is in the well wall, eighty feet below us, so when the knot is on the well lip we shall know we have the right depth" .....*

*"I will get in the bucket," said Elzevir, turning to me, "and this good man will lower me gently by the brake until I reach the string-end down below. Then I will shout out, and so fix you the wheel and give me time to search."*

*"'Tis my place to go , being smaller and lighter than thou"...I said*
*"Art head and heart sure that thou cans't do it lad? Said Elzevir speaking low*
*"Thou art my diamond, and I would rather lose all other diamonds in the world than aught should come to thee."*

# WILLIAM MARINER

When war broke out in August 1914, William Mariner was serving time in Parkhurst Prison. He was an old soldier having served seven years in India with the King's Royal Rifle Corps and five years in the Reserve. He was offered the chance of a reduction of his sentence if he rejoined his unit. So on 26 August he re-enlisted in his old battalion and went to France but was quickly invalided home. He went to France again in 1915 and on 22 May of that year won the Victoria Cross at Cambrai for single-handedly blowing up a machine gun nest which was causing heavy casualties. He was killed on 1 July 1916 on the first day of the Battle of the Somme.

# NED THE DONKEY

*On 1 July 1907 Ned the donkey, whose work on the well-house treadmill at Carisbrooke Castle entertained visitors for 27 years, was shot by the attendant Mr T. McGrotty, after a vet advised he should be destroyed due to old age and infirmity.*

# WILLIAM KEELING

THE COCOS ISLANDS IN THE EAST INDIAN OCEAN WERE DISCOVERED IN 1609 BY WILLIAM KEELING AND ORIGINALLY WERE NAMED THE KEELING ISLANDS IN HIS HONOUR. HE DIED ON THE ISLE OF WIGHT IN 1619 AT THE AGE OF 42 AND HIS DEVOTED WIFE, ANNE, ERECTED A MEMORIAL PLAQUE IN CARISBROOKE CHURCH.

PRINCESS BEATRICE

SIR GODFREY BARING
THE ISLAND'S RECORD BREAKING COUNCILLOR

IW RIFLES
IN FULL DRESS UNIFORM

ROBERT LORRAINE FIRST AVIATOR TO LAND ON THE ISLAND

GLANVILLE FRITILLARY
FOUND ONLY ON THE I.W.

NAB TOWER

In 1736 Michael Morey was found guilty of the murder of his 14 year old grandson. Executed at Winchester, Morey's body was brought back to the Island, coated with tar and hung in a metal cage at Arreton Down. It was left dangling for two years.

*In 1900 twelve cows were standing on a knoll in Godshill when a single bolt of lightning killed the lot. They belonged to Mr Creeth of the Griffin Inn and were valued at £160*

# VECTIS

*Vectis*

was the name given to the island by the Roman Emperor Vesparian in A.D. 43. The name means

"THAT WHICH HAS ARISEN OUT OF THE SEA"

# PUB TALE

Down the *Mill Bay* the *Fisherman's* using his *Spyglass* to see the *Steamer* at *Anchor*. The *Ocean Deck of the Waverley* is *Sloop*-ing as the *Lifeboat* approaches sounding her *Bell*. The *Sun Chequers* the sea and the *Long Shoreman* heads up the *Chine* with the *Cask and Crispin* on his way to the *Three Bishops*.

# VECTIS SUET ROLL

(FROM FARMER'S WIFE MRS DRUDGE'S HANDWRITTEN
BOOK OF FAVOURITE RECIPES)

Make a nice suet pastry with
$^1/_2$ lb self raising flour,
$^1/_4$ lb shredded suet,
2oz sugar.

*Mix to a stiff paste with water, roll out thinly, and
spread with a mixture of 2oz currants, 2 chopped apples,
2 tablespoons syrup or treacle, the grated rind of half a
lemon, and a pinch of spice.*

*Roll up, close the edges firmly, tie in a floured cloth,*
*&*
*BOIL for 2 hours.*

# IN BONCHURCH GRAVEYARD

*Sacred to the memory of Rosa Elizabeth second daughter
of the Revnd James White who died Feb 11th 1848*
AGED 12 YEARS AND 8 MONTHS

*And then two years later*

*Sacred to the memory of Marion Johanna Lilian youngest
daughter of the Revnd James White who died
July 27th 1850*
AGED 2 YEARS

# VENTNOR WEST

THE VENTNOR WEST BRANCH LINE was the
last railway to be built on the Isle of Wight. It ran from Merstone
through Godshill and Whitwell to St Lawrence in 1897 and then
on to the terminus called Ventnor West in 1900. The line ran
through the St Lawrence Tunnel some 619yds long from which
it emerged giving spectacular views of the sea. This line was
unfortunately the first line to be closed during the sacking of the
rail network in 1952.

# REDS VERSUS GREYS

|  | RED SQUIRREL | GREY SQUIRREL |
|---|---|---|
| **SIZE** | | |
| *Body* | 220mm | 260mm |
| *Tail* | 180mm | 220mm |
| *Weight* | 300g | 550g |

## OVER HALF OF ALL REPORTED SQUIRREL DEATHS HAPPEN ON THE ROADS AND THE BLACK SPOT IS LUSHINGTON HILL.

HAZEL NUTS are a favourite food of red squirrels and research carried out on the Newtown copses reported that hazel coppice nut production is highest when the stools are sixteen years old.

Red squirrels have been around for a long time. Fossil remains of the red squirrel have been found on the Island dating back approximately 4,500 years. They were found in the landslip area of the Undercliff area which lies between Blackgang and Luccombe.

*In 1904 the County Motor Identification Mark was deemed as DL. There were just 46 cars and 42 motorcycles on the island.*

49

# INSCRIPTION ON THE SHANKLIN FOUNTAIN

*"O traveller, stay thy weary feet;*
*Drink of the fountain, pure and sweet;*
*It flows for rich and poor the same.*

*Then go thy way, remembering still*
*The wayside well beneath the hill,*
*The cup of water in His name."*
HENRY WADSWORTH LONGFELLOW

The fountain can be found in the Old Village near the top of the Chine.

# LONGDISTANCE PATHS

Tennyson *Trail*
Worsley *Trail*
Hamstead *Trail*
Coastal *Path*
Shepherds *Trail*
Stenbury *Trail*
Bembridge *Trail*
Nunwell *Trail*

All these routes are linear except the Coastal Path which is circular.

THE WOOTTON-QUARR MARINE ARCHAEOLOGICAL SURVEY OF 1992-6 REVEALED 160 INTER TIDAL SITES ALONG JUST 3 MILES OF COASTLINE BETWEEN WOOTTON CREEK AND RYDE WEST SANDS. THREE THOUSAND WOODEN POSTS WERE RECORDED ATTRIBUTED TO NEOLITHIC AND BRONZE AGE FISH TRAPS AND SAXON FISH WEIRS. POTS AND VESSEL FRAGMENTS RECOVERED FROM THE BEACH AND FROM RYDE MOTHERBANK BY OYSTER DREDGERS SUGGEST THE SOLENT TO HAVE BEEN AN ANCHORAGE OF GREAT ANTIQUITY.

**ELEANOR'S GROVE** south of Quarr Abbey is wrongly thought to be the site of a royal burial. It is claimed that Eleanor of Guienne, Henry II's queen, after confinement at Quarr was buried here in a golden coffin protected by strong and unholy spells.

## SMUGGLING SMUGGLERS

*We'll go down among the Needle Rocks,*
*and put them all ashore, O!*
*Back again to Cherbourg,*
*and take in some more, O!*

**Old Song**

| IOW *Speak* | *Translation* |
|---|---|
| Mainland | *Term of abuse* |
| Motorway | *400yards of dual carriageway in Newport* |
| Nipper | *Anyone under the age of 90* |
| I'll get it done for you tomorrow | *Maybe* |
| I'll get it done directly | *You'll have it next year* |
| I'll get it done when I can | *Forget it* |
| Up north | *Cowes* |
| Now you're retiring do you plan to travel? | *Yes, there's lots of the island I haven't seen yet* |

## H.M.S. EURIDICE

On March 22nd 1878 the Euridice was seen off the island, having crossed the Atlantic in 16 days. Bonchurch Coastguard Station noted the ship passing at 3.30pm `moving fast under all plain sail, studding sails on fore and main, bonnets`, Ellen Sewell who lived in Bonchurch sketched the ship `gliding through a green and purple sea`.

The Euridice was just rounding Dunnose Point when a great squall of snow and ice bore down on her. It might have been that view of the accumulation of dense black cloud was obscured by the high mass of St Boniface Down ahead of her, for it seems she was ill prepared for the weather that was about to strike her. Within minutes of being exposed to the freak storm, her masts were broken off and she began to capsize. Of 366 men on board only 2 were saved.

# BONCHURCH PARISH RECORDS

| YEAR | *Marriages* | *Births* | *Deaths* |
|---|---|---|---|
| 1750/59 | 4 | 9 | No record |
| 1760/69 | 7 | 39 | 19 |
| 1770/79 | 5 | 56 | 28 |
| 1780/89 | 8 | 63 | 22 |
| 1790/99 | 5 | 45 | 17 |
| 1800/09 | 5 | 46 | 17 |
| 1810/19 | 5 | 46 | 15 |
| 1820/29 | 3 | 45 | 16 |
| 1830/39 | 11 | 72 | 38 |

As can be seen there was huge village expansion during this time.

# ISLAND POETS

The island home of Algernon Swinburne was East Dene in Bonchurch. The house is set in grounds that sweep down to the sea.

EXTRACT FROM *A Forsaken Garden* **by A.C Swinburne 1878**

*In a coign of the cliff between lowland and highland,*
*At the sea-down's edge between windward and lee,*
*Walled round with rocks as an inland island,*
*The ghost of a garden fronts the sea.*
*A girdle of brushwood and thorn encloses*
*The steep square slope of the blossomless bed*
*Where the weeds that grew green from the graves of its roses*
*Now lie dead.*

# WRECKS

The island black spot for wrecks is Chale Bay, situated between St Catherines Point at the most southerly tip of the island and Atherfield Point on the Military Road. The Bay was dubbed by the *Times* *"The Receiver General of Wrecks for the Isle of Wight"*

The worst single day for wrecks was January 10th 1754 when 5 ships foundered in the night with the loss of ten lives.

## WEATHER EXTREMES FOR THE ISLE OF WIGHT

HIGHEST TEMPERATURE SINCE JANUARY 1969
34.8 degrees celsius
*27th June 1976*

LOWEST TEMPERATURE SINCE JANUARY 1969
- 8.5 degrees celsius
*13th January 1987*

MAXIMUM RAINFALL IN ONE DAY SINCE JANUARY 1969
73.66mm
*10th June 1971*

STRONGEST WINDS SINCE RECORDS BEGAN
104 mph
*16th October 1987*

DEEPEST SNOW SINCE RECORDS BEGAN
Level snow 1 metre deep
*January 1881*

# LOSS OF THE ROYAL GEORGE

*Toll for the Brave !*
*The brave that are no more!*
*All sunk beneath the wave*
*Fast by their native shore!*

*Eight hundred of the brave*
*Whose courage well was tried,*
*Had made the vessel heel*
*And laid her on her side.*

*A land breeze shook the shrouds*
*And she was overset;*
*Down went the Royal George,*
*With all her crew complete.*

*Toll for the brave!*
*Brave Kempenfelt is gone;*
*His last sea-fight is fought,*
*His work of glory done.*

*It was not in the battle;*
*No tempest gave the shock;*

She sprang no fatal leak,
She ran upon no rock.

His sword was in his sheath,
His fingers held the pen,
When Kempenfelt went down
With twice four hundred men.

Weigh the vessel up
Once dreaded by our foes!
And mingle with our cup
The tears that England owes.

Her timbers yet are sound,
And may she float again
Full charged with England's thunder,
And plough the distant main:

But Kempenfelt is gone,
His victories are o'er;
And he and his eight hundred
Shall plough the wave no more.

W. COWPER 1783

# THE ROYAL GEORGE

THE ROYAL GEORGE was a powerful state-of-the-art galleon some 200 feet in length and carrying 100 cannon. Launched in 1756 she had served in many campaigns and was instrumental in the Battle of Quiberon Bay during the Seven Years War defeating the French fleet. That war being over she was then rested in Plymouth for fifteen years having a skeleton crew responsible for her maintenance. She was needed to relieve Gibraltar from blockading Spanish forces and in 1782 she returned to Portsmouth to be loaded with provisions and a full fighting crew. The vessel was found to be in less than tip-top condition and work was required to be done below her water line. There was no time available for her to be repaired in dry dock and so repairs to a submerged water cock were undertaken in the middle of the Solent off Ryde.

On 29th August 1782 full of provisions, crew and their loved ones who were on board to wish them bon voyage, the cannon on one side were pulled and pushed across the deck to the other side, causing the ship to keel over enough to enable the work below the water line to be completed.

This was not sound practice and the weight was too much causing the ship to capsize, flinging 1000+ people into the Solent. Many drowned and their bodies washed ashore off Ryde where they were buried.

# LONGEST CONFINEMENT

*Ann Orchard holds the record for the longest confinement in the workhouse in Newport. She spent sixty years there from 1774-1834 when she died at the age of 101; she was also the oldest inmate. The workhouse is now part of St Mary's Hospital.*

# VICTORIA CROSS HOLDER

## COL HENRY GEORGE GORE BROWNE
### Captain, 32nd Regiment

Won: 21st August 1857 at Lucknow, Indian Mutiny

Sortie against two heavy guns during siege of the Residency

Died at Shanklin 15th November 1912

Buried at St. Mary the Virgin churchyard, Brook.

All Saints
Our Lady & St Wilfrid
St Agnes
St Andrew's
St Blasius
St Boniface
St Catherines

# SOME PARISH SAINTS

St Cecelia's
St David's
St Edmund
St Faith
St George's
St Helen's
St James
St John
St Luke
St Mark's
St Mary
St Mary the Virgin
St Michael and All Angels
St Mildred
St Nicholas in Castro
St Olave's
St Patrick's
St Paul
St Peter
St Saviour
St Thomas of Canterbury

# WARM WINTER WINDS

## *Between the years*

## 1996 – 2005

the wind in January blew for
74 days from the South West;
in August it only came from the
South West on 41 days.

# MAGICAL ISLAND

*"Any man from America or Australia might take one glance at the island as something on a map, and then decide to give it a couple of hours. But you can spend days exploring the Isle of Wight, which, if you are really interested, begins magically enlarging itself for you"*

**J.B.Priestley**

## SEA BREEZE

2 VODKA - 3 CRANBERRY JUICE -
2 GRAPEFRUIT JUICE - LIME PEEL

Shake all the ingredients together with ice and strain into a tall glass

## SIR PETER McDONALD

*Sir Peter D. McDonald won the Isle of Wight seat for the Conservatives in a record eight consecutive Parliamentary elections serving as the island's MP from 1924 to 1959.*

## NOVEMBER IN THE ISLE OF WIGHT
by ALFRED LORD TENNYSON

*November dawns and dewy-glooming downs,*
*The gentle shower, the smell of dying leaves,*
*And the low moan of leaden-colour'd seas.*

# SEVEN HILLS KILLER

This mountain bike Challenge takes place annually on the island between Shanklin and Freshwater.

The Challenge is a mountain bike orienteering event where riders have to plot the best route from Freshwater in the west to Shanklin in the east, taking in 7 way points that are situated on the 7 main hills of the island. The competitors use bridle ways, byways and public roads to achieve their shortest time. The distance is approximately 26 miles and if that's not tough enough some riders do it both ways for a real challenge!

# THE SEA MARK

In 1735 the ways used to transmit information about shipping visible from the island were centralised on the top of Ashey Down. A large white solid stone tower was built visible from miles around. From here the navy sent semaphore messages from the top of a topmast and topgallant mast from a man-o-war to Portsmouth regarding all shipping seen off the island. The landmark is still maintained today although the signalling has ceased.

# PLUTO

**P      L      U      T      O**

THE PIPELINE UNDER THE OCEAN PROJECT WAS DEVISED TO FUEL THE ALLIES IN THEIR NORMANDY CAMPAIGN DURING THE SECOND WORLD WAR. THE PIPELINE RAN FROM SHANKLIN ON THE ISLE OF WIGHT TO CHERBOURG IN FRANCE.

# THE FIRST PERMANENT WIRELESS STATION

In 1897 Guglielmo Marconi and his assistant George Kemp built the first permanent wireless station on the cliffs above Alum Bay in West Wight. From here they proceeded to experiment and refine the equipment, transmitting signals firstly to a tug off the shore and then over to Bournemouth and Poole in Dorset.

Transmissions continued from this site until 1900 when the station was relocated to the southern tip of the island at Knowles Farm in Niton. The commemorative stone at Alum Bay reads as follows:

THIS STONE
MARKS THE SITE OF THE
NEEDLES
WIRELESS TELEGRAPH STATION
WHERE
GUGLIELMO MARCONI
AND HIS BRITISH COLLABORATORS
CARRIED OUT FROM
6TH DECEMBER 1897
TO 26TH MAY 1900
A SERIES OF EXPERIMENTS
WHICH CONSTITUTED SOME OF
THE MORE IMPORTANT PHASES
OF THEIR EARLIER PIONEER
WORK IN THE DEVELOPMENT OF
WIRELESS COMMUNICATION
OF ALL KINDS.

# PRISON ESCAPES

A CLASSIC `knotted sheet` escape attempt was made from Parkhurst Prison on 24th February 1978. Bricks were removed from under the cell floor on the third floor in `A` Wing. The knotted sheet was then secured and dropped into the courtyard outside.

On 3rd January 1995 Parkhurst hit the headlines of the national press when three dangerous prisoners staged a daring escape. Two of the men were Category `A` prisoners and the other one was a `lifer`. They were on the run for seven days during which time they attempted to leave the island by stealing a light aircraft. Throughout this time police manned the island ferry ports hoping to apprehend them. Eventually they were recaptured within a mile of the prison. Their escape contributed to the down grading of Parkhurst Prison to a category B prison.

# GHOSTLY WIGHT

`Ley lines` connect two prominent points in the landscape of prehistoric interest and are said to transmit unseen energy. The Isle of Wight has plenty of unseen energy. It is said to be a haunted island. The island's ghost scene is recorded by one of the leading paranormal researchers Gay Baldwin. She has been investigating and recording sightings of island ghostly activity since 1977.

On the B3401 Carisbrooke to Calbourne road just past the Blacksmiths Arms you can find a lane with a ghostly name. It is Betty Haunt Lane and runs from this high point down to connect with the Yarmouth road.

# PRINCESS BEATRICE

Princess Beatrice was the youngest of Queen Victoria's children and favourite of both parents. She had a long association with the island and married Prince Henry of Battenburg at Whippingham church. She was Governor of the Island for 41 years and a familiar figure at Carisbrooke in the summer.

# THE REV LEGH RIGHMOND

The Rev Legh Righmond, Curate of Brading and Yaverland, became famous for his series of moralistic stories, based on the lives of real islanders, called "The Annals of the Poor." He is not so well known for inventing a hymn and psalm indicator which can be seen in churches of all denominations throughout Britain!

*The Isle of Wight Wave Moth once inhabited a tiny inaccessible ledge off Freshwater cliffs called Roe's Hall Green and nowhere else in Britain. Unfortunately it has not been seen since 1931.*

# THE RAREST BIRD

THE RAREST BIRD TO BE SEEN ON THE ISLAND IS A WALLCREEPER. ON 16 MAY 1985 FOUR BIRDWATCHERS SAW ONE LAND BRIEFLY AT WATERSHOOT BAY BEFORE FLYING OFF TO THE WEST. IT HAS NEVER BEEN RECORDED BEFORE OR SINCE.

# PUB GAME

In the pub game of darts a score of **_eighty-one_** is called by islanders **_deep snow_** after the heavy snowstorm of 1881.

## JULIA MARGARET CAMERON

COMMANDING VIEWS down to Freshwater Bay is Dimbola Lodge, the now restored house of Julia Margaret Cameron, the pioneering Victorian photographer. In a male dominated society she blazed a trail in the art of early photography, creating Pre-Raphaelite images of enduring beauty. She was a forceful woman with, as Jowett noted, `a tendency to make the house quake the moment she enters, but in this dull world that is a very excusable fault`.

She was a colourful character amongst the Farringford Set, who congregated in Freshwater to be near the Poet Laureate Alfred Lord Tennyson at his Farringford home. Julia Margaret's photographs include many of the artists who visited, as well as her famous portrait of the poet himself, which critics referred to as a picture of a dirty monk.

# THE DAY OF THE TRIFFIDS

JOHN WYNDHAM USED THE ISLAND AS THE LAST REFUGE
FROM THE MAN-EATING PLANTS IN HIS APOCALYPTIC
NOVEL 'THE DAY OF THE TRIFFIDS.'

*The world is dominated by monstrous stinging plants;
however the climate and size of the island make it the
perfect place from which to launch a counter-attack. The
location chosen is a large country house in Godshill.*

# MOTTISTONE LONG STONE

The Old English meaning of Mottistone is the moot or talking
stone, implying that in ancient times the site of the Long Stone
above the village of Mottistone was a gathering place for debate.
The ancient monument known as the Long Stone comprises two
stones, one standing and the other lying beside it. The two stones
may be the partial remains of a burial chamber. Connecting
energy Ley Lines can be drawn from the Long Stone to the Cerne
Abbas Giant on the mainland and to Glastonbury Tor.

# TOTLAND TIDES POEM

*When full or new*
*you see the moon*
*the tide's far out*
*in the afternoon*

*But when the moon's*
*at either quarter*
*at tea the beach*
*is under water*

*Six hours the water*
*ebbs away*
*an hour later*
*every day*

*Get down to the beach*
*as soon as you can*
*Time and Tide*
*wait for no man*

# IOW POP FESTIVALS

## 1968-1970

### 1st
*near Godshill, August Bank Holiday* 1968

### 2nd
*a 3day event was at Wootton 1969*

### 3rd
*at Afton Farm, West Wight. A five day event August 1970*

# VENTNOR BREWERY

This brewery has been working since 1840 and uses the spring water flowing from St Boniface Down to make a fine array of traditional ales.

Their trademark is the imaginative names given to the ales produced. These include:

## *Scarecrow Best:*

A full bodied beer at **4.2% abv** that is Outstanding in its Field!

## Hippy High Ale:

At **4.4% abv,** this beer was brewed especially for the Radio One DJ Rob Da Bank's Bestival on the island. It's a light hoppy beer to keep everybody hopping to the music.

## Pistol Night:

at **4.4% abv;** say no more!

## Old Ruby Ale:

**4.7%abv** and named after a colourful local character who would sit in Ventnor pubs giving homespun advice.

## Wight Spirit:

**5.0%abv,** this ale was brewed to celebrate the ever watchful presence of the resident brewery ghost. Beware, this one may creep up on you when you least expect it.

## Anti-freeze:

**5.2%abv.** Anti-freeze winter warmer is only available when the nights draw in. Have you topped up with anti freeze?

## Hygeia Organic Ale:

**4.6%abv.** A new organic beer commemorating Hygeia the Greek Goddess of Health and Hygiene who was adopted by Ventnor in Victorian times when the town was revered as a health spa.

# TIDE TABLE

| LOCATION | RISE IN FEET AT SPRINGS AND NEAPS |
|---|---|
| *Needles Point* | 7 & 5 |
| *Yarmouth* | 7 & 6 |
| *West Cowes* | 12 & 9 |
| *Atherfield Point* | 8 & 7 |
| *Bembridge* | 14 & 10 |
| *Ryde Pier* | 13 & 10 |

# SECOND WORLD WAR

During the air raids of the Second World War many enemy and allied sorties flew across the Isle of Wight. Being so close to the vital Solent harbours of Portsmouth and Southampton, the island was in the line of fire by its very location. On their way back to French air bases across the Channel some German planes crashed; such events happened at sites all over the island including The Hermitage near Whitwell, near Farringford House at Freshwater, Egypt Point in Cowes, Bembridge Down, Bowcombe Down, Cowlease Hill near Shanklin, as well as the many aircraft that came down in the seas around the island.

### AIR RAID STATISTICS FOR THE ISLE OF WIGHT  1940-1941

**KILLED**   **92** men     **90** women     **32** children

The last Air Raid Siren was sounded on the island in
November 1944.

# JOHN VALENTINE GRAY

In Church Litten in Newport stands the Gray Monument.
The inscription reads as follows:

*To the memory*
Of
VANENTINE GRAY
The little Sweep
Interred January the 5th
A.D 1822
In the 10th Year
Of
His Age

THE MONUMENT WAS PAID FOR BY PUBLIC
SUBSCRIPTION
AND ALSO BEARS THE FOLLOWING WORDS:

*In Testimony*
Of
The general Feeling
For suffering Innocence

# NEWTOWN RANDY

*extract from a traditional song:*

I bunched some flowers big as a plate
And dressed me up so dandy o'
To meet my maid by her Mammy's gate
And away to Newtown Randy o'

If anyone had flouted she
Reckon I'd have tanned him o'
The folk they fairly stared at we
A walkin' to the Randy o'

This song continues, telling how the lad bought his maid delicacies of ginger cake and sugar candy, along with a parasol, ribbons and lace. The happy pair danced till their legs did ache at the Randy o'. They saw a dwarf and a proper play and a learned pig called Andy o'. The song ends thus:

I'm a grandfer nigh on four score years
My back and legs be bandy o'
She's sitting there in the chimney chair
The maid I took to the Randy o'

The Randy at Newtown was the yearly fair celebrated on the `vigil, feast and morrow of St Mary Magdalene at La Neuton` granted on the town by King Edward II in 1318 along with a `market on a Wednesday`. The event survived for at least 450 years, but from 1781 its occurrence has been spasmodic. It has been resurrected many times, the last being in 1993.

# CONTRASTING VIEWS OF SMUGGLERS

*"I like a smuggler, he is the only honest thief. He robs nothing but the Revenue, an abstraction I never greatly cared for."*

CHARLES LAMB

## Whereas DR JOHNSON remarked:

*"A smuggler is a wretch who, in defiance of the law, imports and exports goods without the payment of customs."*

The visiting poet DOBELL who was staying near Niton made another interesting observation in 1860. He wrote:

*"The whole population here are smugglers. Everyone has an ostensible occupation, but nobody gets his money by it, or cares to work in it. Here are fishermen who never fish, but always have pockets full of money, and farmers whose farming consists in ploughing the deep by night and whose daily time is spent in standing like herons on lookout posts."*

## MANOEUVRING HOOTS

When manoeuvring at sea the following Hoots are recognised:

**1 short blast** - altering course to starboard
**2 short blasts** - altering course to port
**3 short blasts** - going astern

**2 long + 1 short** - overtaking you on starboard side
**2 long + 2 short** - overtaking you on the port side
**Long-short-long-short** - agree your signal

*Newport surgeon, Thomas L. Waterworth, thought Blackgang could grow into a Spa town to rival Cheltenham when he discovered a chalybeate spring at Sandrock in 1808. He erected a dispensary selling bottles of water for half a crown, but it never really got off the ground, perhaps because the brown liquid tasted like ink and made you nauseous!*

## BY THE WIND SAILOR

*Very occasionally* thousands of By the Wind Sailors are washed onto island beaches during bouts of bad weather. They originate in the tropics and are blown off course by ocean storms. They are technically not jellyfish but a complex aggregate of individual polyps, each with a special function – reproduction, digestion and defence.

Their horny sail and 10cms long bodies resemble components from electrical circuits dotted with silver solder and vibrant blues that catch the light. Once beached their tiny sails wither and this magical visitor decomposes.

# COMPTON BEACH COW

A woman from Cowes had a lucky escape when she narrowly escaped being crushed by a falling cow. She had been sunbathing at Compton Bay beach and, picking up her body board, was walking towards the sea when the cow, which had been grazing in the cliff top field, fell 50 feet to the beach. The dead cow was covered with a tarpaulin until the farmer could remove it at low tide.

# A BOATHOUSE ON STILTS

In a boathouse built 15 feet above the stony shore of Myrtle Bay in Ventnor a lady nicknamed 'Britannia' lived for 38 years. She became a well-known local eccentric. The boathouse built on stilts was originally constructed for Ventnor Swimming Club in the mid 1800s.

By 1958 the hut, still with no water or electrics, become so badly damaged that the Council, who had made her frequent offers of a more suitable home, evicted her. She died four years later in her early eighties.

# ISLE OF WIGHT RACES

At Ashey in fields adjoining the station, horse racing takes place in the spring. Since early in the 1900s flat races, hurdles and steeplechases have featured. Race day includes the Isle of Wight Grand National and the Ashey Scurry. In Victorian times mainland competitors and horses arrived by boat. They were stabled at Ryde and then raced. Queen Victoria is said to have watched the event from the comfort of her steam train carriage and today spectators are still able to travel to the races by steam train from either Smallbrook or Havenstreet stations.

## BIGGEST WALKING FESTIVAL IN UK

IN EIGHT YEARS THE ISLAND WALKING FESTIVAL HAS GROWN INTO A VERY LARGE EVENT, BOASTING OVER 200 WALKS IN 2006. WITH WIDE ISLAND COVERAGE THE ISLAND'S WELL KEPT FOOTPATHS OFFER GREAT VARIETY FOR WALKERS AT ALL LEVELS. THE NOVELTY WALK FOR 2006 WAS THE SPEED DATING WALK, WHICH ATTRACTED A LOT OF MEDIA COVERAGE. OTHER FAVOURITES INCLUDE THE LEISURELY ACCESSIBLE WALKS FOR FAMILIES AND WHEELCHAIR USERS, AND THE GRUELLING ROUND THE ISLAND IN 24HOURS CHALLENGE.

**Did you know**

the lone rock standing off Freshwater Bay is known as Stag Rock on account of the day when a deer escaping from a pack of hounds leapt onto it for safety?

# DRAW BRIDGE

Yarmouth has throughout its history felt threatened by the sea. The causeway of the River Yar on whose banks the town is built, stretches inland towards Freshwater on the south coast. At Yarmouth Castle built in Henry VIII's reign the surrounding ditches were pumped by engines to keep them free of water. In 1609 buttresses were constructed to shore up the castle walls and in 1664 when the marsh embankments were constructed the town had a draw bridge.

# NEEDLES LIGHTHOUSE

THE OLD NEEDLES LIGHTHOUSE WAS BUILT ON THE CLIFF-TOP IN 1781. THE PRESENT DAY LIGHTHOUSE STANDS ON GOOSE ROCK AT THE END OF THE NEEDLES ROCKS AND WAS CONSTRUCTED IN 1858.

# FOOTPRINTS FROM THE PAST

Hanover Point in West Wight is a location rich in evidence of our pre-historic past. On the rock shelf (and only visible at low tide) are the trail of footprints left by a young iguanodon as it foraged for food amongst ancient trees. The surrounding fossil forest is clearly visible and those with eyes like a hawk can, with luck on their side, find fossil teeth, fools gold and other fossil wonders.

# ISLAND MOTTO

# ALL THIS BEAUTY IS OF GOD

# VIEW POINT DISTANCES FROM VENTNOR

MADRID 1147KM

LE HAVRE 195KM     ALDERNEY 120KM

PARIS 317 KM

PANAMA 8612KM     LUXEMBOURG 534KM

WASHINGTON 6095KM

DUNKERQUE 258KM     POOLE 57KM

CHICHESTER 40KM

CARDIFF 174KM     LONDON 125KM

SOUTHAMPTON 40KM

PORTSMOUTH 25KM     MANCHESTER 332KM

# ARTHUR HENNESSEY

In January 1946 Arthur Hennessey became the first convict to reach the mainland after escaping from an island penal establishment.

# RAPUNZEL'S TOWER

THE FOLLY KNOWN AS APPLEY TOWER ON APPLEY SEAFRONT AT RYDE HAS AN AIR OF THE FAIRY-TALE TOWER THAT IMPRISONED RAPUNZEL. THE FOLLY WAS BUILT BY SIR WILLIAM HUTT IN THE MID 1800s AND WAS A FAVOURITE DESTINATION STROLL FOR THE ELEGANT VICTORIAN LADIES OF RYDE. THE FRENCH INSCRIPTION ABOVE THE CASTLE DOOR TRANSLATES AS `TO WISH IS TO BE ABLE` ( TO MAKE IT POSSIBLE) OR AS WE MIGHT SAY `JUST WISH AND IT WILL COME TRUE`

# FLOATING BRIDGE

At the tidal head of the River Medina where the waters swirl into the Solent a floating bridge clanks between Cowes and East Cowes. This chain ferry is one of only a few remaining in the country and `service frequency and crossing time depends on river traffic, tides and weather conditions`

# MONK DESIGNS NEW ABBEY

The old abbey at Quarr was suppressed during the dissolution of the monasteries under Henry VIII in 1536 and left in ruins. In 1901 a group of persecuted French monks left France and settled on the Isle of Wight. Initially they inhabited Appuldurcombe House at Wroxall but then moved to Quarr House outside Binstead. Here they started on the construction of a new abbey. The building, designed by Dom Paul Bellot, one of the monks, is very distinct in style and constructed of brick. It became an independent priory in 1925 and an abbey in 1937.

# OLD JACK

At Dunnose Point, south of Shanklin there is a large natural cave known as `Old Jack`. This cave was used extensively by the local smugglers. It could store 5000 gallons of spirits. Another cave at Bonchurch, just up the coast from Dunnose was also known as `Old Jack`. The smugglers were out to confuse everyone including the Revenue Men.

## SOURCE TO SEA

The Yar River Trail is a 19 mile route following the Yar River from its source in Niton to where it reaches the sea at St Helens Duver. Along the route a total of twenty distinctive stone way markers tell you how far you are from the source and from the sea.

## THE LARGEST LANDSLIP IN EUROPE

Gault
clay (known
locally as blue slipper) is one
of the causes of the land instability found
especially on the southern coast of the island. The Landslip and Undercliff reputedly form the largest landslip in Europe.

## THE GNOMON

*In 1851 the gnomon was erected on the Esplanade in Ventnor.*

*A gnomon is a stationary 'arm' that projects shadow as on a sundial.*

# HIGHEST POINT

St
Boniface
Down rises
steeply from sea
level to **745** feet. It is
the highest point on the island.

## A LIGHTHOUSE THAT WAS TOO TALL

In 1840, soon after its completion, the height of the lighthouse at St Catherine's Point on the southern tip of the island was 120 feet. It was soon found that the light was forever in sea mists and fog and therefore invisible from the shipping it was designed to protect. In 1875 the height was reduced to 90 feet. The lighthouse became fully automated in 1998.

# GURNARD REGATTA

As well as racing yachts at the Gurnard Regatta there was also a dog race. Owners would take their pets out to sea and then drop them over the side to see which dog swam to shore in the quickest time. In recent years the R.S.P.C.A. have disallowed this event.

# MEAN MAN

TITUS TUTTON OF NITON REPUTEDLY GAVE HIS CHILDREN MONEY TO GO TO BED AT NIGHT. IN THE MORNING HE WOULD THEN CHARGE THEM FOR THEIR BREAKFAST.

# THE VALLEY OF APPLES

*Appuldurcombe House draws its name from the `valley of apples` in which it nestles. The imposing facade seen today in the village of Wroxall was part of a classic structure built by the Worsley family between 1773 and 1782.*

THE ORIGINAL GROUNDS WERE LAID OUT BY 'CAPABILITY' BROWN.

# BEACH FOOTBALL

FOR THE PAST FIVE YEARS the annual beach Football Championships have taken place. This is Europe's largest beach soccer tournament. In 2006 32 teams competed, all kicking up a fair amount of sand. The Wightlink Cup is presented to the winners.

# COWES WEEK BEGINNINGS

Back in 1826 the Royal Yacht Club in Cowes introduced racing for cups into the Cowes Regatta; this became very popular, a popularity that grew and grew. Cowes Regatta itself stemmed from the local pilot cutters receiving their licences, and in 1815 local yachts followed the cutters in a water parade. In 1826 the Club advertised a yacht race for a gold cup valued at £100, a race that was open to club yachts of any rig or tonnage; the entry fee was £2. The race took place with seven entrants. Today the number of yachts racing at Cowes during the internationally popular Cowes Week exceeds 1,000.

# RAILWAY AT VENTNOR

THE RAILWAY ARRIVED IN VENTNOR IN 1866.

&

CLOSED EXACTLY 100 YEARS LATER IN 1966.

# OLDEST CARNIVAL

Ryde's first recorded Carnival was held in 1888; it consisted of a torchlight procession through the town featuring the town's Volunteer Band, the Fire Brigade and a mass of townspeople in fancy dress. The Isle of Wight Observer reported: *"Such a stirring procession has never been seen before in Ryde"* The parading townsfolk depicted the Kings and Queens of the realm along with a tableau of the reigning monarch Queen Victoria. Today a flourishing initiative has taken Carnival on the Island to new heights.

# NAVIGABLE RIVER

The River Medina starts its journey to the sea from the south of the island near Chale Green and eventually reaches its goal on the north coast between Cowes and East Cowes. Along its route it passes through interestingly named areas including The Wilderness and Blackwater. At Newport it becomes navigable down an ever widening estuary. There are four and a half miles of boating to be enjoyed between Newport and the Solent.

# COWES CANNONS

**There are 22 cannons on the esplanade at Cowes in front of the Royal Yacht Squadron building. These are fired to start the many races that take place each year, and originate from the Royal Adelaide; they were presented to the Royal Yacht Squadron by Edward VII.**

# SOURCES

The following publications are among the many sources consulted.

**Edmund Venables,**
A GUIDE TO THE ISLE OF WIGHT, 1860.

**Marian Lane,**
PIERS OF THE ISLE OF WIGHT, 1996.

**D.J.Quigley,**
THE ISLE OF WIGHT RIFLES, 1976.

**Adrian Searle,**
THE ISLE OF WIGHT AT WAR, 1939-1945, 1989.

**David L. Williams,**
WINGS OVER THE ISLAND, 1999.

**John Mackett,**
THE PORTSMOUTH — RYDE PASSAGE, 1970.

**Douglas Phillips-Birt,**
WATERS OF THE WIGHT, 1967.

**Ken Phillips,**
SHIPWRECKS OF THE ISLE OF WIGHT, 1988.

**J.C.Medland,**

SHIPWRECKS OF THE WIGHT, 1986.

**Martin Simpson,**

FOSSIL HUNTING ON DINOSAUR ISLAND, 1998.

**David Martill & Darren Naish, ed,**

DINOSAURS OF THE ISLE OF WIGHT.

**R.K.Sheridon,**

LORDS, CAPTAINS & GOVERNORS OF THE
ISLE OF WIGHT, 1975.

**Frank Morey,**

GUIDE TO THE NATURAL HISTORY OF THE
ISLE OF WIGHT, 1909.

**Oliver Frazer,**

THE NATURAL HISTORY OF THE ISLE OF WIGHT, 1990.

**Maurice Leppard,**

BLACK ON WHITE.

**Shepard & Greening,**

READ ALL ABOUT IT.

**Shepard & Greening,**

AN EVERYDAY STORY OF COUNTRY FOLK.

# ACKNOWLEDGEMENTS

We would like to thank the following individuals and
organisations:

The I.W. County Press, Islander Magazine, I.W.
Council and I.W. Tourism, County Library Service,
I.W. Ornithological Group, I.W. Natural History and
Archaeological Society, Ventnor Heritage Museum, Joanna
Jones and Fanny Oglander for permission to reproduce
recipes, Mrs Lavers for permission to reproduce material
from Jack Lavers' *Isle of Wight Dialect*.
Brian Greening & Bill Shepard.

ISLAND MOTTO

# `ALL THIS BEAUTY IS OF GOD`

Published By **Coach House** Publications

see more titles available from www.coachhousepublications.co.